great mistak[e

newts in white satin

potential mistakes in the jungle:

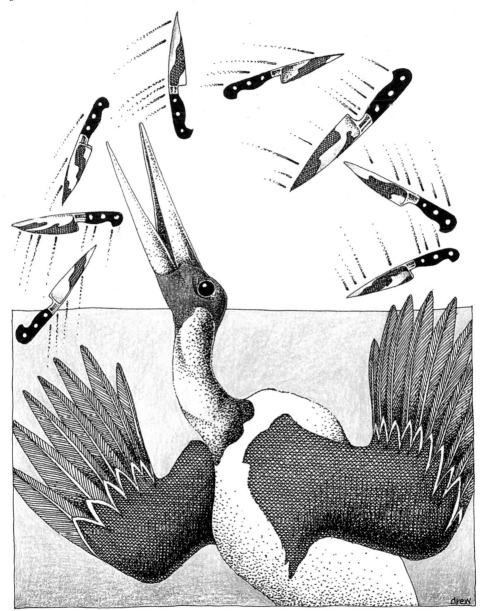

careless stork costs lives

great mistakes of history:

gibbon's decline and fall

Great Mistakes of Civilisation

Mankind's Mistakes and Faux Pas

gnome
or mister nice guy ?

Drawings and Verses
by
Simon Drew

ANTIQUE COLLECTORS' CLUB

Important Fruit in History:

ALEXANDER THE GRAPE

to my wife Caroline
and
everyone who
made helpful suggestions

© 1996 Simon Drew   ISBN 1 85149 246 1
World copyright reserved

British Library Cataloguing-in-Publication Data
A catalogue record for this book is available from the British Library

Published and printed in England by the Antique Collectors' Club Ltd., Woodbridge,
Suffolk IP12 1DS on Consort Royal Satin paper from Donside Mills, Aberdeen

great coincidences of nature:

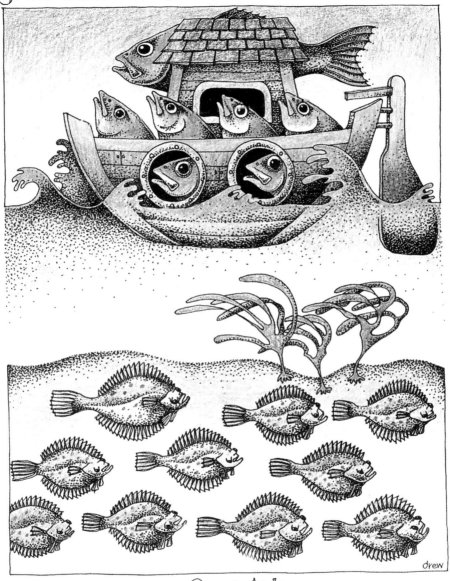

Carp Ark
(near ten rillington plaice)

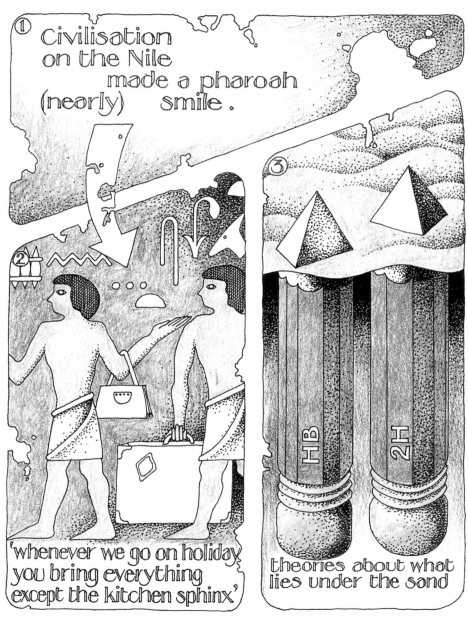

① Civilisation on the Nile made a pharoah (nearly) smile.

②

'whenever we go on holiday you bring everything except the kitchen sphinx'

③

theories about what lies under the sand

...yet more northerly
⑨

Pity King Arthur's knights were fakes. Did King Alfred like burnt cakes?

⑩

a knight of the round table searching for the holy quail

⑪

peculiarly

Monarchs of England slow and wild? Looking fierce but meek and mild.

⑫

ethelred the ovenready

great mistakes of history:

CUSTER'S LAST STANDARD POODLE

drew

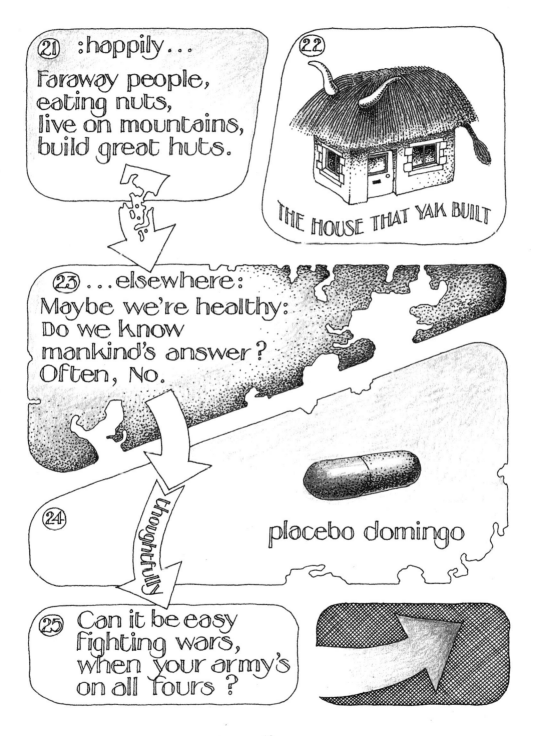

21 :happily...
Faraway people,
eating nuts,
live on mountains,
build great huts.

22 THE HOUSE THAT YAK BUILT

23 ...elsewhere:
Maybe we're healthy:
Do we know
mankind's answer?
Often, No.

24 placebo domingo

thoughtfully

25 Can it be easy
fighting wars,
when your army's
on all fours?

THE SPINACH INQUISITION

finally

31 Nothing else happened
worth recall.
(Just a few things,
mostly small.)

THE END OF HISTORY

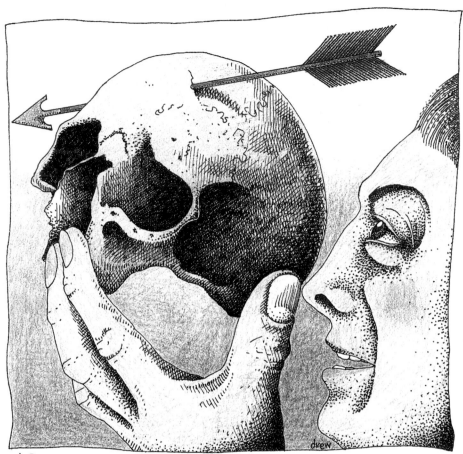

"Alas poor Yorick,
he knew William Tell."

william shakespeare
with his tortoise andronicus

simon drew, dartmo... devon, UK.

the hentertainer

the hendangered species

the
henvironmentalist
(also known as
'green with henvy')

duck
chair

duck
turpin

bombay
duck

simon drew dartmouth devon UK

20

xon of
uck
reen

capon capon
duck

stool
pigeon

drew

21

Robin Hood and his merry hen

last mango in Paris

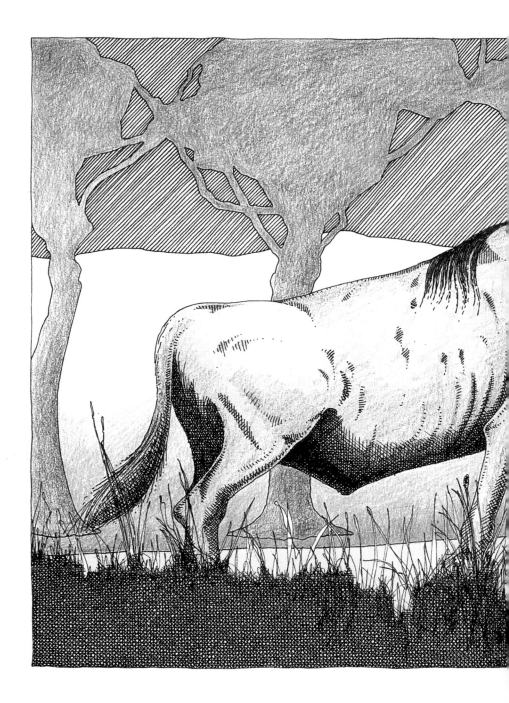

annie get your gnu

great mistakes of biology:

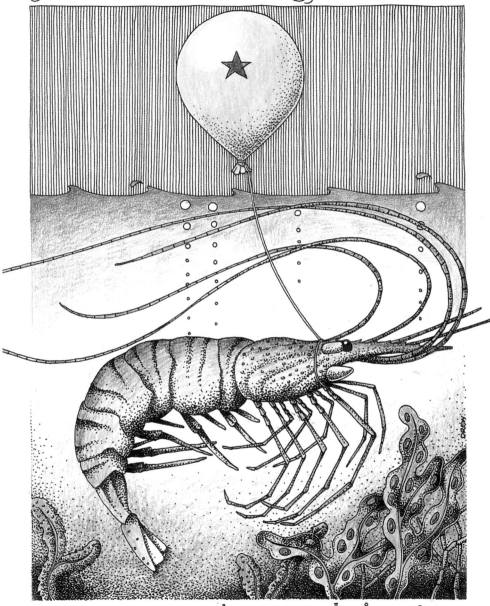

prawn under a wandering star

little known ancient vegetable relics:

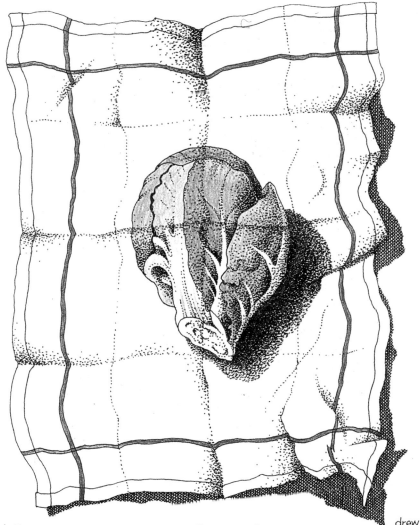

drew

When you have no faith in beans,
If you don't believe in greens,
If you're left in any doubt:
Come and see the Turin Sprout.

great mistakes of history:

the spotted doge of Venice

29

drew

VINCENT'S BIRTHDAY

vincent was so happy
he was grinning from ear to

great mistakes of the bible:

the salmon on the mount

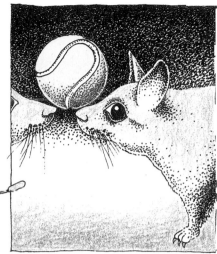

the acts of the opossums

Lot's wife –
turned into a
pillar of salt beef
sandwiches

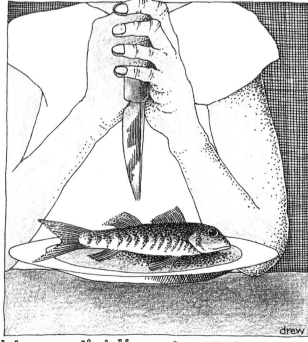

Moses dividing the red mullet

JACK THE VEGETABLE RIDES AGAIN

A tale of fear and intimidation from the 17th c.
This story from Ancient Basingstoke has never
been told before.

"It's Monday," all the people shout;
children laugh and run about.
Soon they'll see a real sprout:
the Vegetable Express is due in town.
But just when things are going well,
where's that hint of cabbage smell?
What's that ringing warning bell?
Something's come to let their spirits down

Carrot's disappearing.
Someone's interfering.
Who's the man who's got a sack?
Jack.

Where's that cauliflower?
Who's got all the power?
Who's the thief who's dressed in black?
Jack.

(Never trust a vegetarian)

JACK OF VEGETABLES   DREW

the story of....

King Canute (a conservative with a small sea).

drew

great coincidences in nature:

Edgar   Rice   Burrows

pope springs eternal

at the chicken liver party   simon drew dartmouth

chicken livers

tequila mocking bird

42

all animals are inkwells
but some are more inkwells than others.

the reason that the first world war started:

great mistakes of history:

a druid attempts henge gliding

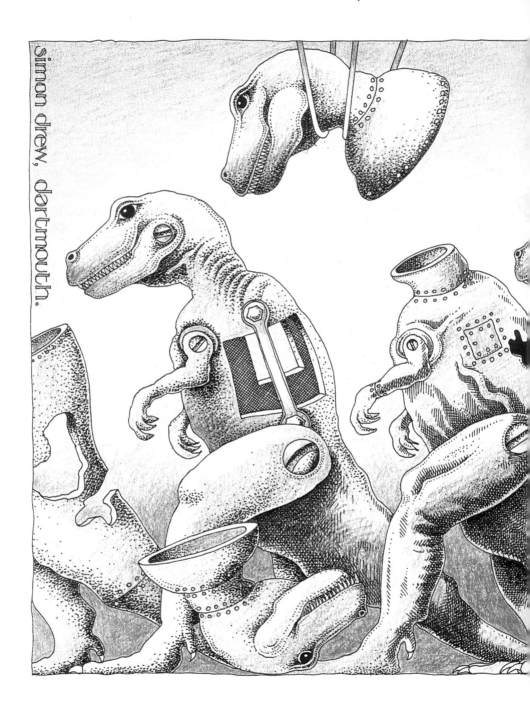

simon drew, dartmouth.

46

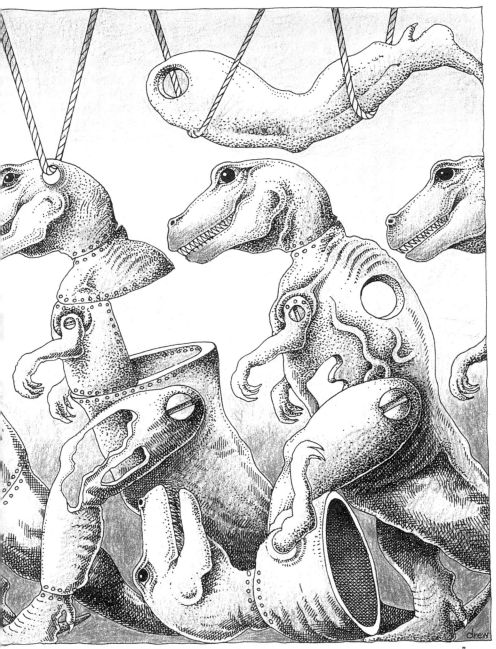

tyrannosaurus wrecks

there are four types of people:

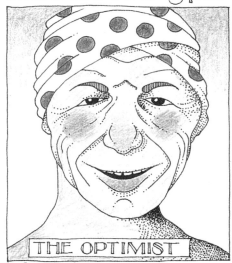

THE OPTIMIST

There's always
someone worse off
than yourself

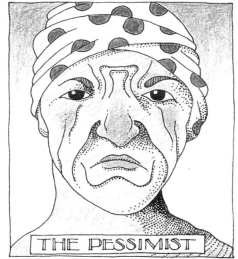

THE PESSIMIST

There's always
yourself worse off
than someone

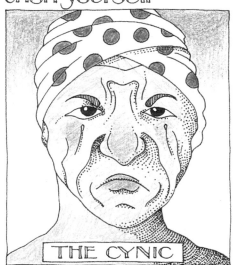

THE CYNIC

There's always
someone

THE GERMAN

Worse off than
yourself someone
always there is